Dedication

This book is in honor of the 12 million immigrants that passed through Ellis Island and in support of the approximate 45 million immigrants who currently reside in the United States.

Statue of Liberty from the habor with
view of Ellis Island in the background.
Circa 1895.

Ellis Island may have been the offical entry point for
immigrants to enter the United States, however it
wasn't their first stop. Many arriving ships were to
big to dock at Ellis Island so they first docked in
Manhattan where American citizens and first and second
class passengers were allowed to enter the country
after only a brief inspection.

Italian family en rounte to Ellis Island.
Circa 1905.

Steerage passengers were herded onto ferries for them to be taken to Ellis Island to be processed. This stopover in Manhattan was not without corruption. Sly immigration officials were known to take bribes from immigrants trying to avoid going through the inspection process on Ellis Island.

View of ferry boat as it nears Battery Park.
Circa 1902-1913

There were times when so many people were unloaded in Manhattan that they were made to wait several days and several nights for these small boats to carry them to the island. There were up to 850 staff to help process up to 10,000 passengers in a single day. Many of these staff members were interpreters.

Immigrant Station, Ellis Island, with
ferry docked at adjacent pier. Circa
1902-1913.

Between the years of 1892 and 1954, over 12 million
people went through this processing center. Of all those
people only 2 percent were deemed unfit to become
citizens of the United States. They were then deported.
Extreme sickness or legal issues could be reasons for
deportation.

A social worker explains to a group of
immigrants some of the technicalities
of becoming an American. Circa 1926.

Upon arrival, each immigrant was labeled with their
name and the name of the ship which they arrived on.
It is falsely believed that large amounts of name
changes happened during the processing on Ellis Island
when, in reality, most of those changes or mistakes
happened overseas when leaving their home county. The
shipping company was responsible for recording the
passenger's name on the ship's manifest.

Italian family looking for lost baggage.
Circa 1905.

Everyone entered the main building through the baggage room where all bags, trunks and luggage were kept until after the medical tests were done.

Mother and child si outside the
detention cell. Circa 1905.
Men were seperated from the women and children
until after medical evalutions were complete.

Jew from Russia at Ellis Island. Circa 1905.
As soon as immigrants entered the Registry Room
doctors were looking for initials signs of
medical or mental issues. Chalk marks on their
clothing were used to signal further tests were
needed.

Immigrants undergoing medical examination.
Circa 1902-1913.

As people climbed the stairs to get in the long winding
line doctors were already watching from afar for signs
of illness. Each initial examine was only 7 seconds long
per person. If medical problems were found that were
treatable they may be sent to the islands hospital to be
treated. Some incurable or disabling ailments were
reason for deportation at the expense of the shipping
line that they arrived on. Tuberculosis and insanity
were among the conditions that were looked for.

Interpreter and recorder interviewing
newcomers, Ellis Island, New York.
Circa 1908.

Inspectors would question the immigrants in the Great
Hall to determine if they should be granted admittance
to America. Inspection could take an average of 3 to 5
hours if papers and documents were in order. However, it
could take days to get through the inspection because of
the amount of people trying to get into the country.
Questions such as: Where were you born? Have you ever
been convicted of a crime? How much money do you have?
If their answers differed from what was on the ship
manifest they could be detained for further questioning.

A bearded immigrant appearing before a
board of inquiry. Circa 1902-1910.

Those who were detained lived in the dormitory room
until their case was reviewed in the Hearing Room. Their
stay could be as short as a few days to as long as a
month until they learned whether they would be allowed
to enter the U.S.

Taft, Williams, and three others on
Ellis Island. October 18, 1910.

President Taft visited Ellis Island to see conditions
first hand. After his visit he made efforts to pass new
laws and change procedures. Foremost he set to change
the procedure of separating husbands from their families
believing this to be "…worthy of utmost condemnation."
He believed if immigrants were treated justly that they
respond in kind.

William Williams at his desk. Circa
1902-1910.

William Williams was the federal commissioner of
immigration for the Port of New York from 1902-1905 and
1909-1914. His office was located on Ellis Island.
Williams worked very hard to eliminate corrupt practices
at Ellis Island going as far as to have people dress up
as fake immigrants to go through the process. This
helped find the inspectors that were taking bribes and
other illegal practices. Williams fired all officials
found to be participating in such scams.

Immigrants being served a free meal at Ellis Island.
Circa 1902-1913.

Women and children who were traveling without a man would
be detained until their safety was guaranteed by a
relative that was already in the United States. Some had
to wait days for a letter or telegram to arrive as
documentation.

Mid-morning lunch at Ellis Island.
Circa 1926

The food service on Ellis Island was also fraught with issues and corruption ranging from outrageous prices to serving rotten food. While some meals were served for free most had to be purchased by poor starving immigrants who had just spent two weeks to several months on a ship. This picture depicts an attendant bringing a milk lunch, a great improvement over the prunes and prune sandwiches that were previously offered.

Immigrants detained at Ellis Island take
time to be happy. Circa 1926.

There was no organized recreation, so the immigrants
supplied their own. Here they are playing the accordion
and dancing.

Lined up at teller's windows marked
money exchange. Circa 1902-1913.

After being approved and ready for travel going north,
south and west. Some stayed in New York while many
traveled to far places for opportunity or to meet with
family.

Passed and waiting to be taken off
Ellis Island. Circa 1902-1913.

The first floor of the building became known as the
kissing post. It was where family and friends waited for
loved ones and celebrated the relief of such a long
journey to America being over. Although, for many, their
journey continued on to all different parts of the
country.

Dutch Children.

Unaccompanied children were not unheard of. In fact, the
first person in line the day Ellis Island opened was an
unaccompanied minor by the name of Annie Moore, she was
15 the day she arrived. She brought with her two little
brothers. Some of these children had family awaiting
their arrival. Though many others did not. Some children
who didn't have anyone to claim them were kept in deten -
tion until a local missionary or private citizen would
agree to take guardianship of the child.

Greek soldier. Circa 1911.

Many immigrants traveled on foot, by horse or by train from long distances to get to the port where they would board a ship to America. Some were escaping poverty and religious intolerance from places such as Italy, Poland and Russia. The ships they traveled on carried as many as 3000 people, many speaking different languages.

Gypsy Family.

In 1909 there were laws in place that required each immigrant to have at least $20 before they were allowed to enter America. The government wanted people to be able to support themselves until they were able to get settled.

Lithuanian woman with colorful shawl. Circa 1926.
Many European immigrants made this long journey attracted
by the abundance of land and jobs with booming
industries. They were hoping for a higher standard of
living.

Three women from Guadeloupe.
New York Mayor Fiorello LaGuardia previously worked on Ellis Island. He was the son of Italian Immigrants and was fluent in Italian, Croatian and Yiddish and served as a translator while he went to law school. He later represented many immigrants in deportation cases. His name may be familiar to many in the Queens airport, LaGuardia Airport.

Albanian soldier.
1907 holds the record for most immigrants in a year at
1,004,756.

Bavarian man.
There is a belief that 40% of American citizens today
can trace an ancestor to Ellis Island.

Cossack man from the steppes of Russia.
Although only 2% of immigrants were turned away that
amounted in 80,000 people giving the island the nickname
'The Island of Tears'.

Jewish grandmother. Circa 1926.
Ellis Island was closed and in limbo for 20 years until
1976 when it was opened for tours. Renovations and the
building of a museum took another 15 years to come
together and reopened in 1990. Ellis Island, The Gateway
to Freedom, now receives approximately 3 million
visitors a year.

Family Tree

See if you can discover when your family immigranted to the United States

Other titles by Twigs Greenpage

Coloring Books

Accessible Coloring Book
Humorous Hummingbirds
Scardy Pardy and Friends - Boston Terrier Coloring Book

Prompt Journals

Zen as F*ck
What's up Monkey Butt
Today We Garden
30 Day Drawing Challenge Journal

ADHD Resources

Daily Report Card
Keep Calm and Start Doing
My ADHD Adventure

Many Blank Journals and Notebooks are available as well.